This book belongs to
_____

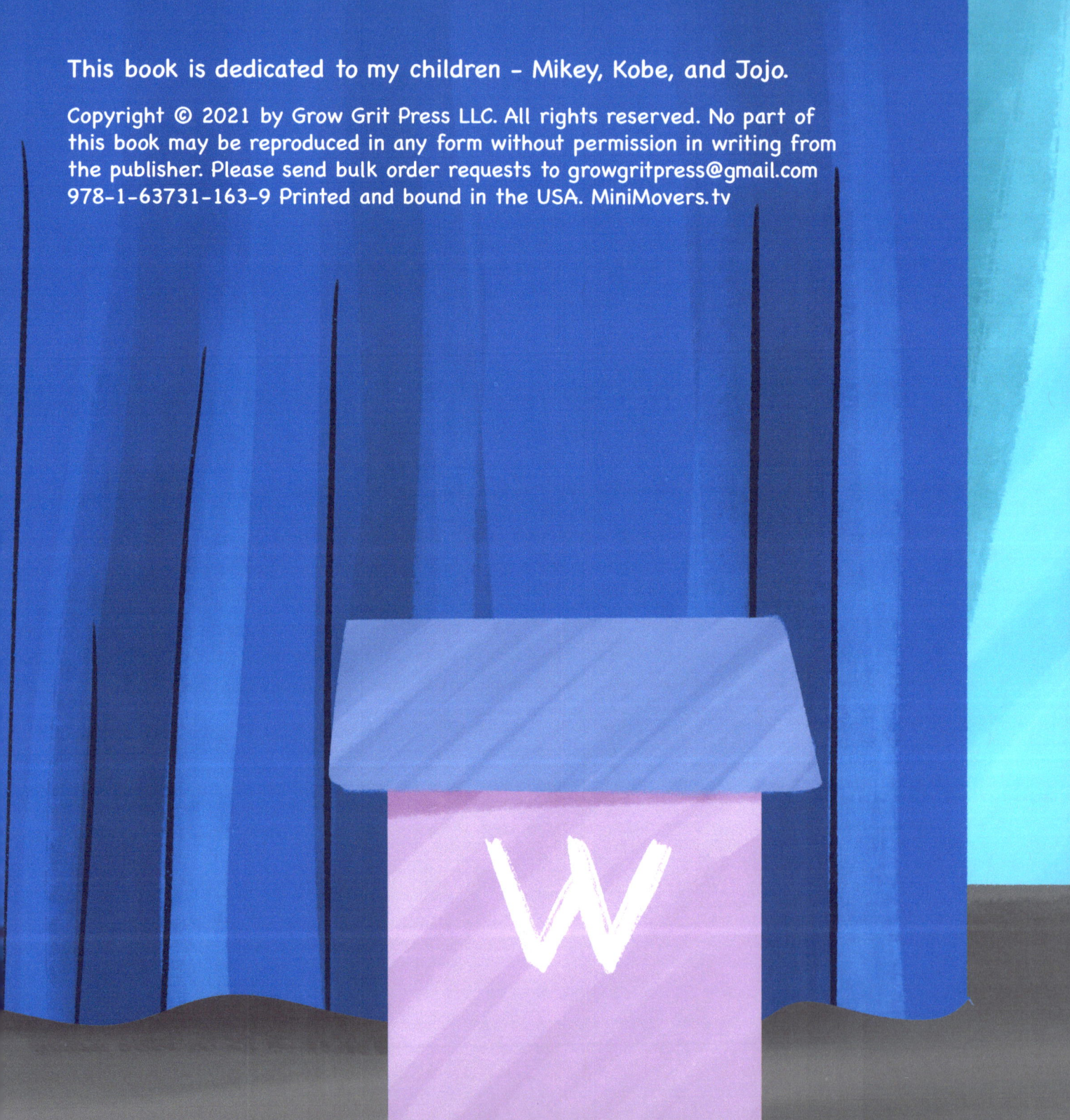

This book is dedicated to my children - Mikey, Kobe, and Jojo.

Copyright © 2021 by Grow Grit Press LLC. All rights reserved. No part of this book may be reproduced in any form without permission in writing from the publisher. Please send bulk order requests to growgritpress@gmail.com 978-1-63731-163-9 Printed and bound in the USA. MiniMovers.tv

Indra Nooyi

By Mary Nhin

Pictures By
Yuliia Zolotova

Hi, I'm Indra Nooyi.

Growing up, I played guitar in a rock band and had big dreams. For a girl in India, at the time, that was considered strange.

I was driven and received college degrees in physics, chemistry, and mathematics.

I wanted to study at Yale School of Management in the United States.

But, at first, my mom didn't want me to go.

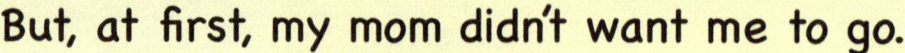

I grew up in a Hindu household with a mother who said I'll arrange a marriage for you at eighteen. But she, also, said that we could achieve anything we put our minds to and encouraged us to dream of becoming Prime Minister or President.

My parents have always supported me, and, eventually, they allowed me to move to America to study.

After graduating, I worked in business giving advice to companies. I joined a company called PepsiCo and I worked my way up to CEO!

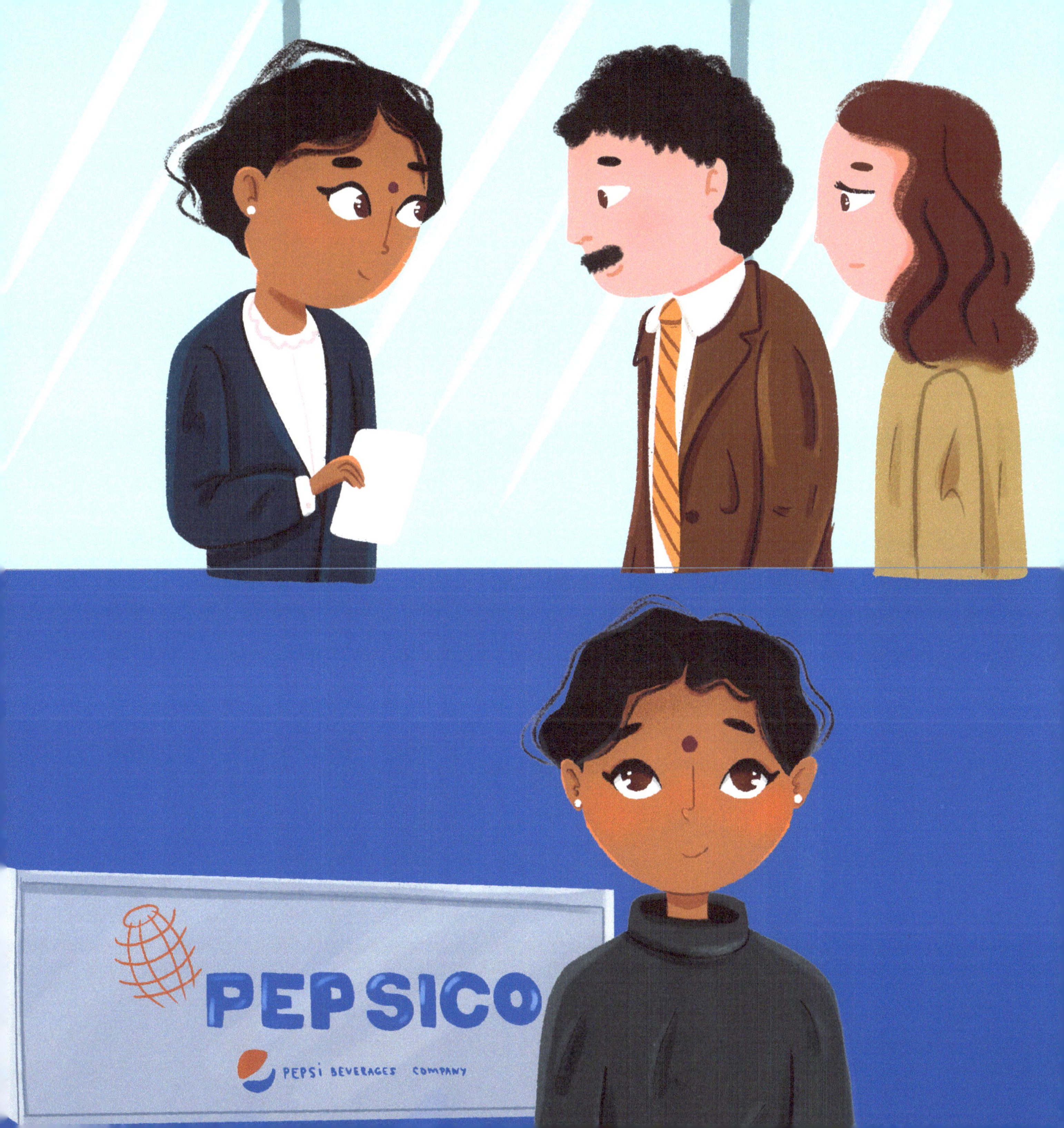
PEPSICO
PEPSi BEVERAGES COMPANY

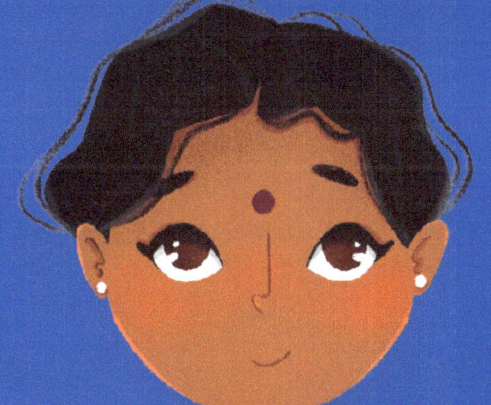

I had already made lots of great decisions by then, but as CEO I wanted to make a big change. I wanted to focus on healthier foods. My new strategy, Performance with a Purpose, grouped our products into three categories:

'Fun for You' such as potato chips and regular soda,

I purposely moved away from junk foods and into healthier alternatives with the aim of improving the healthiness of even the "fun" offerings. In 2015, I removed aspartame, an artificial sweetener, from Diet Pepsi, furthering the shift towards healthier foods.

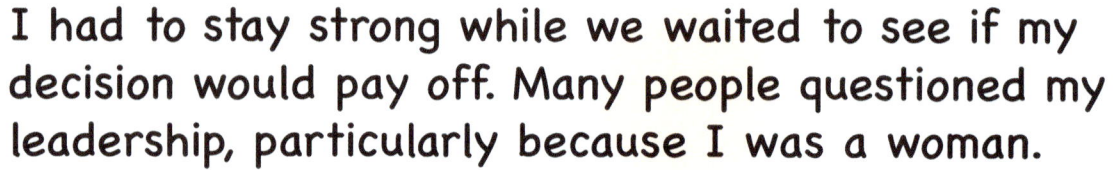

I had to stay strong while we waited to see if my decision would pay off. Many people questioned my leadership, particularly because I was a woman.

POST

WHAT IS INDRA THINKING

In fact, I almost lost my job, but I wasn't worried.
I knew in my heart this was a good decision.

As part of the Performance with a Purpose, I also focused on environmental concerns and sustainability, redesigning packaging to reduce waste, conserving water, switching to renewable energy sources and recycling.

Finally, the results came in and there was the profit to prove that I had been right.

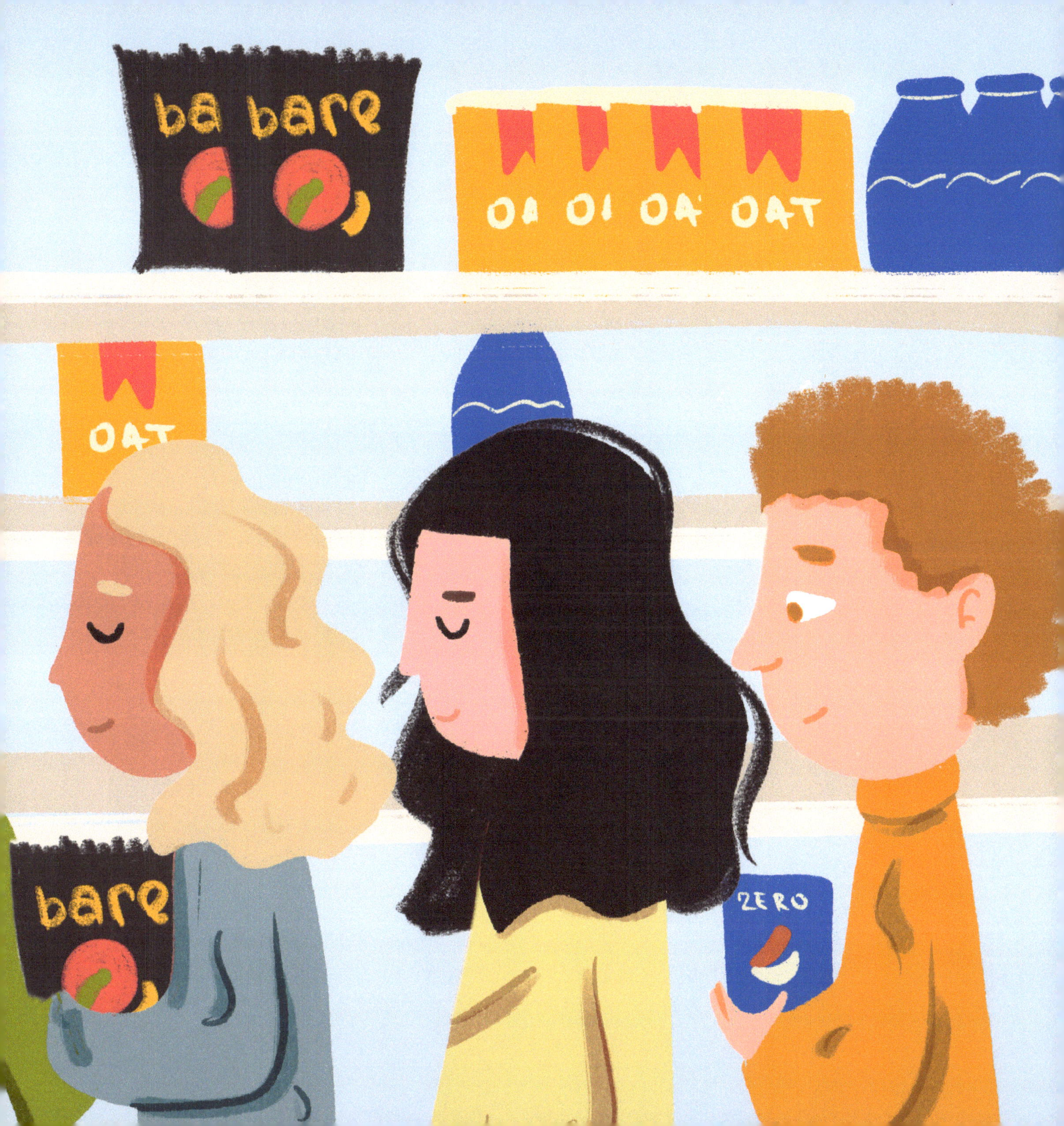
ba bare
OA OI OA OAT
OAT
bare
ZERO

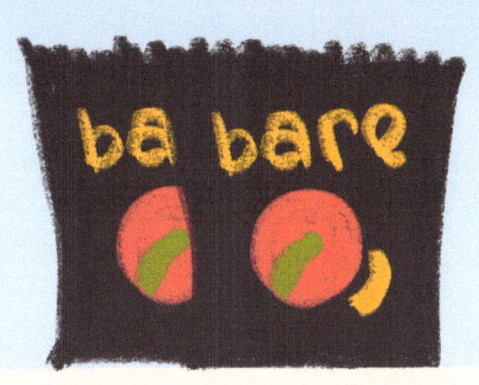

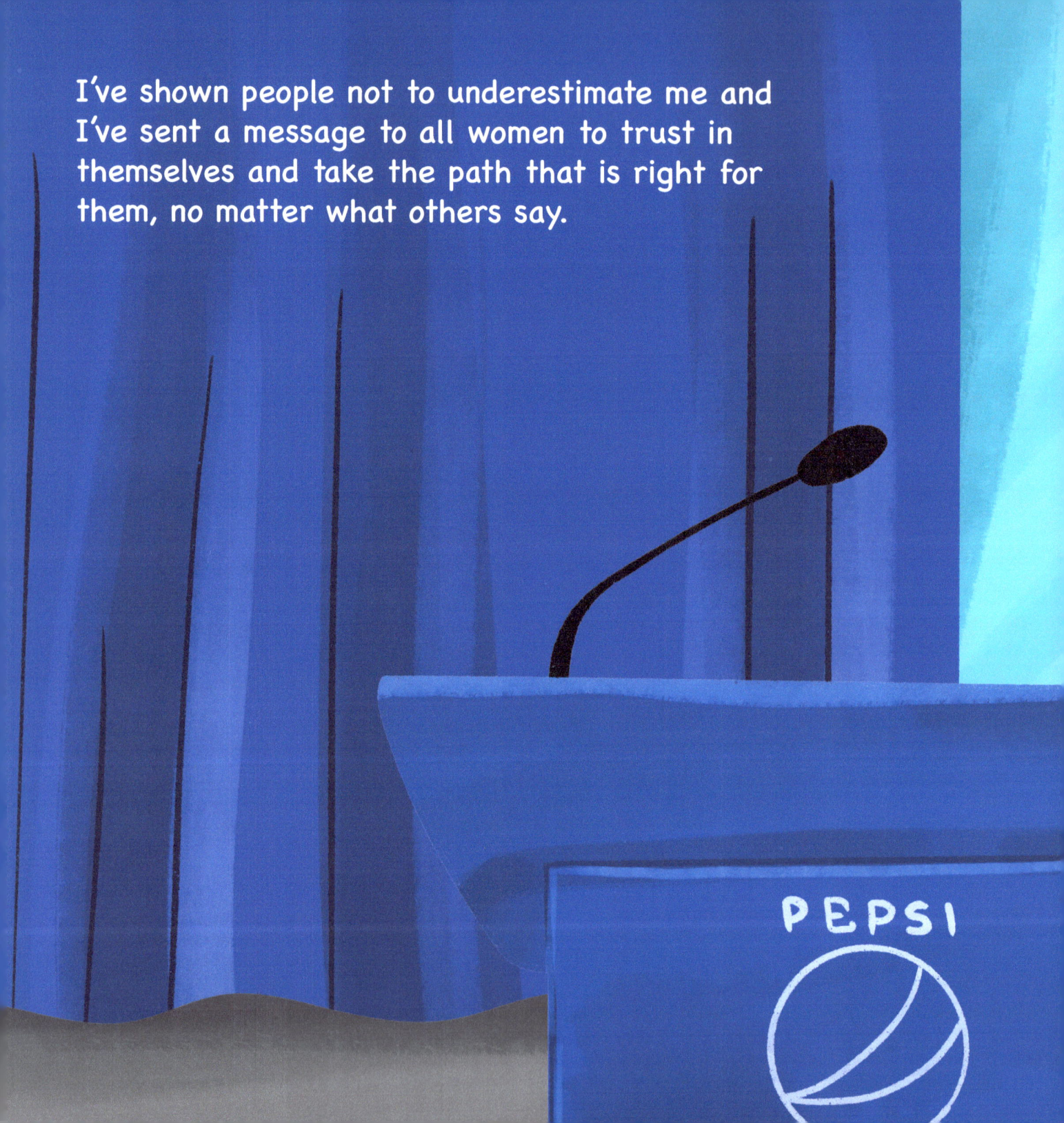

I've shown people not to underestimate me and I've sent a message to all women to trust in themselves and take the path that is right for them, no matter what others say.

Timeline

2006 - Indra becomes CEO off PepsiCo

2007 – As CEO, Indra gives PepsiCo a new direction

2012 – Indra risks losing job as PepsiCo doubts her

2017 – Indra is ranked among the world's 100 most powerful women for the 9th year running

2018 – Indra is named one of the best CEOs in the world

minimovers.tv

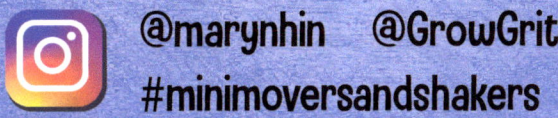 @marynhin @GrowGrit
#minimoversandshakers

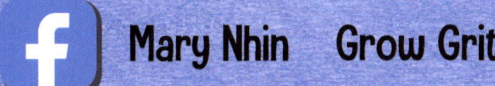 Mary Nhin   Grow Grit

 Grow Grit

www.ingramcontent.com/pod-product-compliance
Lightning Source LLC
Chambersburg PA
CBHW041523070526
44585CB00002B/54